A CATERPILLAR INTO A BUTTERFLY

A Caterpillar into a Butterfly

Catherine Johnston

Printed and bound in Great Britain by:
Book Printing UK, Remus House, Coltsfoot Drive, Woodston,
Peterborough PE2 9BF

Dedication

Thank you to my family:-

- My husband John, who has been with me through my depression. He's my friend and rock.
- My mum, dad and sister, Eileen, who aren't with us. They are waiting in heaven for me. They were a big part of my life.
- John's mum who has laughed with us and is still a good friend.

Thanks to my friends:-

- Norma, Anne and Brenda and her husband who have helped us a lot.
- John and Christine for blessing us and our family.
- Joyce, who believed I could achieve this book and who taught me many things. She made me strong in God.
- Alan Reeve and his wife who mentored John and me.
- Barry and his wife, Tina.
- Ladies from Women Aglow, Rochdale and beyond.
- My friends at our new church, who have helped me achieve this book.

May God bless each person who has been involved in my life. Each one means something to me. You are all special.

Most of all, I thank God for my life in Him. It is through Him that I can do all things. Everyone can have dreams and desires. If you wait on God he will give them to you.

Curses and Blessings

I have known God for twenty five years and have been married to John for the same length of time. John and I are blessed. We have four wonderful children. I prayed for grandchildren and within six years we had nine! My prayers were answered!
I am going to tell you about my life, including my family, and what God has done for me.
My life has not been easy. There have been times when I just wanted to give up.

Some people don't know about blessings and curses. Blessings are positive. They are words spoken to you or about you that are good. They encourage you. Encouragement cheers you up. This is a blessing. Curses are the opposite. They pull you down. They have negative results in your life.

When people tell you, "you're no good, you won't and can't do anything with your life, you're thick, you're a nobody" they bring discouragement. These things weigh you down and you feel guilty and ashamed. Name calling has the same effect. Such things are curses. Relatives and others called me names. They told me I was hopeless and an idiot and that I would be all my life. I believe what they said about me. I was cursed. God is different. God is truth and he blesses you with good things. Blessed be the name of the Lord. Yes, I am still disabled and have had a hard life, but because God is with me, I am an overcomer. I am no longer under those curses. I have written poems about my life and spoken in halls and churches. I am married to a wonderful man of God, who is my rock, my friend and also a pillar of strength when I need it.
There is a book called "if you want to walk on water then get out of the boat." Fear stopped me getting out of the boat of self-doubt, low self-esteem and shyness. I would stand behind John. I would let him be my mouth. If I was asked to read from the Bible or even pray out loud I'd burst into tears. It was my friend Norma who made me look in a mirror. She told me that God had made

me. He was pleased with me. I was his princess. I was beautiful in God's eyes.

God looks within a person. God knew me before I was born. He set me apart. He knitted me together in my mother's womb. I am fearfully and wonderfully made. God doesn't look at my disability. He looks at my ability – a woman who can make a difference.

The devil comes to steal and destroy. The devil had stolen my boldness. I also thought nobody would love me again.

We sometimes go through things we don't like. We can let our past stop us from moving into a good future. But God comes to give joy and life to the full. God knew my future even when I didn't. He had John planned for my life before I was born.

God's blessings are for all of us. We have food and drink. We have clothes. We have a roof over our heads. We have friends who love us. We are blessed. You are never too old or too young for God. All his promises are true.

"For I know the plans I have for you," says the Lord, "plans to prosper you and not to harm you, plans to give you hope and a future." (Jeremiah 29.11).

God knows your comings and goings.

I will bless those who bless you and whoever curses you I will curse. All people on earth will be blessed through you. We are told to bless those who curse us so they will feel shame when we give them a drink of cold water. God is in control, we aren't.

God won the victory when Jesus rose from the dead.

Proverbs describes the noble wife as:

"She is clothed with strength and dignity; she can laugh without fear. Her children arise and call her blessed; also her husband praises her. Many women do noble things but you surpass them all."

God's promises are good and He does not to leave us. When Elizabeth met Mary who was pregnant with Jesus she said, "Blessed is she who has believed that what the Lord has said to her will be fulfilled."

God remembers his promises forever. God's promises are for me, my children, my grandchildren and their grandchildren.

My Younger Years

I was five years old when I started school. From the first day the children called me names because my leg was twisted. It would drag a bit. These names hurt me. They say "sticks and stones may break my bones but words will never hurt me." Well, this is a lie. Words do hurt.

On the first day of school, the teacher met me at the door. Mrs Wilde was her name. She showed me to the classroom. I was shown to a table which I shared with another girl and two boys. There was a pencil and a book with my name on it.

At play time I stood on my own and the other children all stared at me. I went into the play tunnel to hide. I sat alone in the tunnel until another girl came. It was the girl who sat on my table. She asked if she could sit with me. Later, we swapped lunch. Her name was Anne. My Mum always packed my lunch up. Anne and I would stay close. Every day we swapped crisps as she didn't have much.

Anne came from a large family of nine. Sometimes Anne came with nothing to eat. My Mum had brought us up to share and be grateful. Anne was the only one who stayed with me. We played together, and also cried together. Anne also got picked on because she was different. She didn't have good clothes. We sometimes swapped clothes. Sometimes my Mum helped her mum.

When it was games I sat out as I couldn't do the things others could. I always fell over when I tried to run. Sometimes the teacher and Anne took my hands and ran with me. The teacher lifted me over things. Yes, I still came last but I never gave up. When it came to sports day, Mum made me sit out. She thought she was doing good but I hated it because I felt left out. My Mum always thought she was protecting me. I know Mum loved me. She didn't want me to feel embarrassed. Instead, I felt rejected and alone. At times I felt stupid when the children kept looking at me.

The name calling went deep within my heart. I believed what was being said. When I became a Christian I learned that Jesus took all my shame and guilt on the cross. Jesus took it all.

Mum went to the Church of England. My Dad was a Catholic and so I went to Catholic school. My parents never argued over it.
Dad had a drink and gambling problem. He often came home drunk. My parents ran a pub. Sometimes I dreaded my Dad coming home and seeing what he was like.
I have a brother Robert who is twelve months younger than me. We had a sister Eileen who was fifteen years older than me. Eileen was my Mum's daughter from her first marriage, but she was "our" Eileen.
My parents were always busy behind the bar. When I was born I was often left in the pushchair, so Eileen usually looked after me. Eileen also looked after Robert. She took us to town on the bus. Eileen would take me as her own. She taught me to walk and talk. I'm told I didn't walk until I was three, because of my leg. An early memory is going to the fair and Eileen tying me on a roundabout. People thought she was my mum and that my Mum was my grandma. My Mum looked too old to be my Mum! She was forty when she had me.

We moved out of the pub when I was six. We moved to a council estate. It was on the estate that Mum met Peggy. She was married and Scottish. She liked singing and bingo. Mum and Peggy went to the bingo club together. Peggy got Mum a cleaning job at the club. Mum always worked hard and took Robert and me with her. Mum mopped the floors while Robert and I went on the stage and sang! Mum never left us alone at home, just in case Dad came home drunk.

There were two bedrooms in our new house. Robert and I slept in the same room in twin beds. Mum and Dad slept in twin beds in their room. When Robert and I got a bit older we swapped rooms. Mum slept in my room in her bed, me in mine. Dad and

Robert shared the same bedroom. We didn't have enough money to rent privately so we stayed in the same house for years.

My parents had big problems. Once, Dad came home and threw a big chair at Mum. Sometimes Mum would get us out of bed in the night and take us to our auntie's house. We stayed there for weeks.

One auntie was into spiritualism and my other auntie went to church. There was a third aunt who read tea leaves. It was no wonder we were confused about religion. Robert loved the spiritualism because he knew what was going to happen before it did. He also read tea leaves. He was into anything weird. Robert was a laugh. He always cracked jokes. Once he put a three penny bit into a church collection and got two back for his change! Sometimes he would faint in church. I thought that was one way of getting out of it. I couldn't do it. He was a clever monkey.

Our Eileen never went to church with us. When she was young she was in the Girls Brigade.
She was busy with her own children. Eileen had a girl and a boy and lived for them. She always helped others in need. She baked for people and helped those in the same boat as she was. She always had people in her house and some people would call her for help. She wasn't rich. She said she had her settee on bricks as one of the legs had broken off.
Every weekend I went to Eileen's house. I stayed Friday to Sunday. I can remember one day I got so fed up that I went into Eileen's house. I hid in the cellar so Mum couldn't find me. I was OK until I saw a rat. I screamed! Mum found me and made me go home.

Eileen was a life saver. She taught me a lot. I could tell her things that I never shared with Mum. I take after Eileen with a caring heart.

Once a month my Gran came on a Sunday. She was Catholic. We had to go with her and Dad to church. She was funny. Gran always smiled at us and gave us goodies. She had a spare room with toys in. She bought things from the market and stored them up. So we always got toys from her. She gave some of the toys to other people who hadn't anything at Christmas time. My Dad always called Gran names, but if anyone else did he'd go mad.

My Granddad died when I was five but I can still remember him. He was kind and soft. He was bald. We could do anything to him. My Granddad loved children. At first, my grandparents thought they couldn't have children so they adopted a three month old boy. A year later they had my Dad. My Gran said that's when they knew prayer worked. My Gran was 90 years old when she died. She would have lived longer but some lads burgled her one night and held a gun to her face. She died the day after. It wasn't the same after that.

Robert started school the year after me. We stayed close. Dad took us to school in his taxi and brought us home again. The teachers all knew Dad well.

Dad only drank at night because of his work, but weekends were crazy.
I was five when I had my tonsils out and I can remember Dad coming home drunk. He came in the kitchen and pulled the cooker over. The dinner was boiling on top of the hob. As I tried to run my leg twisted and the cooker fell on me. Peggy came over. She took me and mum to the infirmary to have me checked over. I was OK, just shocked. I ended up at Peggy's house for ice cream while the kitchen at home was sorted out. In fact, I stayed at Peggy's that night. Peggy was good to Mum, and Mum was good to her.

One Christmas my two aunts and my Gran came for tea. Dad came in very drunk. Robert was so mad with him. Dad kept nipping my Mum's legs so that they were sore. She was standing near the fireplace. She grabbed the closest thing she could. It was a crucifix. She hit Dad so hard his eye bled. Then Mum just walked back to the kitchen. Robert called an ambulance. It was mad. The ambulance came. Dad's eye wasn't too bad. The ambulance men told Dad to sober up. Dad went to his friends to sober up. I can still remember these things. I always went to my bedroom so I was out of the way. I didn't want the cooker on top of me again.

These situations continued until we started secondary school. Robert did judo. One day Robert threw Dad down the stairs when Dad went to hit Mum again. Another night Dad was very drunk. So drunk he couldn't walk home. Robert had to get a friend to help him drag Dad across the road. When he got home Mum threw him in the bath, turned on the cold tap and left him in it. This had to stop. Where was God in this?

Although we went to a church school we did not know Jesus. We were made to go to church. It was a duty. I didn't understand it all. I went to church to shut my Gran up.
Gran was a strong woman. I can remember there was no meat on Fridays, we only had fish.
One Easter, Dad said, "I bet the Pope's having steak."
Gran hit my Dad. We all laughed at him, but not at Gran.

Mum took us to the church next to our school. At the church, Mum met Alice. Alice had a daughter with Downs Syndrome. Alice told Mum things would get better if she went to church with her. Mum got involved with the church and went to meetings with Alice. Things started to get better in our home. Dad still gambled a lot but didn't drink as much. I think Robert had warned Dad. The weekend Robert and his friend had dragged Dad home was so shameful for Dad. The following week Dad had to go to work with bruises and cuts on his head and face. We now went to church on Sundays. For the walk of witness we got dressed in white. After the walk, we went for a meal in town. We went into a Chinese restaurant every year. Dad treated us all, including Alice.

Each year, Alice took us to a holiday camp in Blackpool. One year, Robert won a competition. I came second. Between us we won vouchers for a free holiday for the following year. Mum and Dad danced. They won the competition – we got free drinks for a week plus £10 in cash. It was a lot then, so we all went into Blackpool for the day. We were friends with Alice for many years, until her death. Her daughter then had to go into a convent where nuns looked after her.

Across the road from us lived a couple who we thought were posh. They had roses and other flowers in their garden. We would laugh because they were called Mr. and Mrs. Rose! Robert played football and when the ball went into their garden, Mrs Rose picked up the ball and took it in her house. Dad had to go and ask for the ball back. Mr Rose was nice though. He gave the ball back straightaway.

One month we didn't see Mr Rose. The hearse was outside his house. Robert, being outgoing, went and knocked on their door. He asked Mrs Rose what was up. She said Mr Rose had died and it was his funeral. Robert then asked if he could see Mr Rose. He turned to Mrs Rose and said, "He don't look well does he?" She had to chuckle.

This was when we made friends. We came closer to her. Robert went shopping for her. After that, she sometimes watched us while Mum went cleaning. When it was school holidays we went to her house for tea.

My Mum sometimes cut some roses and put them in a vase in her window. We still joked about the name!

I joined the Brownies and Robert joined Cubs. I liked Brownies. There was a bit of God input, but I didn't understand it. With both aunties into other stuff we did a bit of everything really.

Our Eileen still came to see us and we often played outside with her two children.

My balance wasn't too clever as my leg was still twisted. I fell over a lot when I was off balance. If a dog barked I'd be put off balance. IT only needed a firework to go off and I would fall over. A car could just blow its horn and I'd fall. Robert would say, "watch the matchstick". If anyone else tried saying it, he would tell them off. I was satisfied playing inside whereas Robert loved playing football outside. I sometimes helped Mum with shopping.

Dad owned a taxi so sometimes I went with him. Sometimes we went out on Saturdays for the day. My friend, Anne, from school would come with me and sleep over. She would stay till Sunday night. Dad started to get better and took us anywhere we wanted to go. I got him running Anne home to fetch her clothes to sleep at my house. Sometimes I stayed at hers.

Anne and I stayed in the same class all through infant school and became good friends. My Dad knew her dad. Anne's dad sometimes gave us eggs as he had some chickens. He also had a horse. Sometimes he let us go and see the horse although I didn't go on it. At other times Mum took us all to the park. When it was Bonfire Night Mum did black peas and toffee. People on the street put money together for fireworks. Afterwards, Robert and his friends camped out for the night to watch the fire go down. I'd go in. I didn't do camping. I watched from the bedroom and feel safe. Robert was more for outdoors than I was. Eventually, Dad put water on the bonfire to make sure the fire was out and all was safe.

When children called me names, Robert stuck up for me. He always got into fights. Robert started middle school a year after me. It felt strange him not being at the same school as me.
I liked middle school. Some of the teachers were nuns. I got friendly with one of them. She told me that someday I would make a difference. I would help people in the same boat as myself. She liked my stories. I'd write stories and dramas for people and poems for others.
One nun was my mentor. I could tell her my problems at any time. She liked me and saw something in me. Both these nuns told me to believe that God would take me to places. I needed to lift up my chin and never be ashamed again.
One of the nuns did music, so I played the tambourine. Anne played viola. I loved music. I think it was because I heard so much music around me. Eileen played it all day long when she was cleaning.
We sang over the sound of the hoover. Anne always had music on at her house. My Dad and Mum danced when they were younger. They won medals in competitions.

Anne was in the same class as me. I also knew some others at the school.
I played table tennis at school. I liked it because you didn't need to do much running. Anne helped me. Everything was alright until some girls started to bully me. One day the girls threw eggs and flour at us. Dad collected Anne and me from school that day. Once again this made me go back into my shell. I was at middle school for two years.

Then I started high school. I got into smoking as my friends were doing it. I didn't want to feel left out. My balance wasn't too bad so I walked to school and back. Dad sometimes came when it rained hard. He also dropped Anne off.
One day we got caught smoking at school. I couldn't run off. As punishment, the teacher made me cut grass with scissors, which I didn't mind.

I hated maths but I liked English. I was hopeless at French. I didn't pass any exams when I left school.

Robert got into bikes and sometimes stayed at his friend's house. His friend went out with my niece. I wasn't into bikes but I would go with Robert to Eileen's. Robert went out with my nephew. I sat with Eileen as she had fits.
Eileen helped an old man by baking him pies. Eileen had lumps on her legs, so he helped her. The old man helped when Eileen had to go into hospital. While Eileen was in hospital her house got burgled. It was a nasty thing to do.

When I left school I didn't go to church any more. I thought, "What's the point?"
I was sixteen when I left school but had no job for a while. Peggy worked in a mill. She asked them if there was a job for me. Sometimes during school holidays I went with Peggy and came home with a bit of money. Mum had taught us to save, which I did. Robert liked to spend his money.
I kept going to Eileen's house at weekends. After a few months we started going to the pub on a Friday. I didn't drink much, only a shandy. Eileen wasn't allowed alcohol because of her medication. I drank a bit more when I went out with Anne, but only an odd one. I'd had enough of seeing what drink could do.

Robert went to live with my niece's boyfriend. I got his bedroom. Mum and Dad went into the other bedroom. I hadn't seen Mum and Dad show affection to each other until I left school. Mum had kept strong and stubborn all the time Dad had hurt her.

With the money I had saved I bought a record player from Anne and I also bought a citizen band radio (CB) I made new friends through it. My nick name was Flower Bud. Robert was Mr Nice Guy because he was nice to his friends. Robert's friend who worked on the buses was named Bus Stop.

We met loads of lorry drivers through the CB. I never met up with anyone unless Robert was with me. We directed lost lorries coming off the motorway.

Dad also had a go. Dad's name was Joe, so he got called Joe Baxi. Mum never had a go. Eileen had a go on the CB and started to sing on it. She was a mad sister. She always made me laugh, just like Robert did.

I got a babysitting job. I was friendly with the little girl's mother. I took care of the girl once a week. I was paid £5. It was a lot of money for a sixteen year old. I bought records and gave up smoking for a while. Mum showed me how to save.

Sometimes Mum let me look after the little girl at our house. We would have a chippy. Robert went on his bike to collect it. Mum went on the back. She was braver than me.

At that time, Dad worked nights, so it was peaceful at home.

I went out with Anne once a week, dancing at a youth club. The youth club was on our Estate. It was good fun. I was small for my age and passed for fifteen. I felt safe at the club. We only had fruit juice. No alcohol was allowed. Dad came for me at the end of the night.

One day we had our nephew round. We were in the garden when it started to rain. My nephew pushed me and I fell in the mud. Everyone laughed at me. Nobody thought there was anything wrong with laughing at me. Mum went mad at my nephew. From then on I started to stay in the house again.

I became very depressed and just played records in my bedroom. I went down for meals. Sometimes Anne came and tried to get me out. Robert had a bike but I was not good at balance so I didn't ride. I had dolls and clothes.

Eventually, Eileen got me to go to her house for a while. She always got me out as I felt safe with her. She was my rock. I went home after about two months at her house.

I needed money. Mum didn't have much money as Dad gambled a lot.

Dad spent money on Bingo and betting shops. Anything left he gave to Mum. At times Mum waited until Dad came home drunk. He went to bed to sleep it off. Mum would take money out of Dad's trouser pockets while he slept. Sometimes Mum got me to do it.

Mum said she might as well take the money as Dad would only spend it on the machines. When Dad had sobered up he thought he had spent the money on gambling and drinking. He wasn't any the wiser that Mum had taken it.

Once, Robert bought Dad some cigars. Dad put them in his drawer and forgot about them. Robert knew this, so took the cigars and rewrapped them and gave them back to Dad for Christmas. Dad thought he had smoked the previous cigars. Robert got away with the trick twice. Robert laughed so much Mum realised what had been happening.

Mum enjoyed getting chocolate and a bottle of stout with the money she got from Dad. Sometimes she went to the local lake in a taxi and bought a fish. We would sit on a bench enjoying it. Mum always made sure we were fed first then she would have her treat. Mum said she felt guilty when she bought something nice for herself. She always bought her clothes from charity shops.

My Workplace

I thought the job would never come. The phone rang. It was Peggy. She had got me a job folding blankets. It wasn't the best of jobs but it was a start in life. It was better than being on the DHSS and always asking Mum for money which she did not have.

Work started at 8am. On the first day, Peggy and I got on the bus. Mum had given me some butties. I was so nervous. The boss met me and shook my hand. He showed me what to do. There were breaks when workers could go and smoke. I joined others smoking in the ladies toilets.

I worked a week in hand. I had some money saved from babysitting. I bought things for my butties and paid for my bus fares from my savings.

I also found another woman who needed a babysitter. Her baby was born on my first pay day, so this was special.

I went home with my first pay packet and gave it all to Mum. There was £12. Mum gave me £4 back. I bought records and a baby-grow for the new born baby. The baby hadn't got a name yet.

I loved looking after the baby girl because this got me away from people who called me names. I didn't fall as much although my leg was still twisted. I taught the toddler to walk on the bowling green. She was lovely. People didn't mind her going on the grass when the bowlers were having their dinner. I relaxed when the baby was in her pram. Eventually the regular babysitting stopped. I kept in touch as every two months I cared for the little girl till the family moved away.

I was a home loving girl really, but this didn't last. I met a lad who worked at the mill. We got chatting and started going out together.

A few weeks passed. We had a relationship and went out drinking. I wasn't a big drinker, but I did like a drink. I didn't smoke.

The relationship with the lad at the mill ended but I found out I was expecting. This meant I needed a sit down job. The women at the mill looked after me, although the lad left his job. When I needed to sit down because I felt faint the women would get the boss. On Fridays we went to the pub for dinner. It was a treat. We all loved Fridays. We had an hour break instead of a half hour. We had dinner and a drink. I'd have a shandy.

Dad took Mum and me to the clinic. The midwife called us in. I wondered why. She told me I was having twins. I was eighteen and with my parents. I was shocked. I felt alone again. Anne rang me and Eileen was there for me.
I had two months to go before the birth. I was fit really except for a few aches. The boss let me go home early now and again with pay.
The woman at work played with the Ouija board and wanted me to join in to see what sex the twins would be. I decided to get involved even though I knew I shouldn't. I went on the Ouija board to see what I was having, but I felt so sick I had to go home. I didn't find out after all.

When I went to the doctors I was told there were only two weeks left and that I must take it easy. I went back to work for the last day. The women took me out for a meal, gave me flowers and kissed me goodbye. I left to have my twins.
I went to bed one night thinking of the women. How kind they were to me. About 5am that morning I had a really strong back pain. I got up and went downstairs. Robert was sleeping at home that night. He was on the couch so I tried not to wake him up. As I went into the kitchen, blood started coming out of me. I screamed! Robert came into the kitchen. He was white. He shouted for Mum and rang for the ambulance. It took ages to arrive.
Peggy came over when she the ambulance. She was in her nightdress. She tried to help my Mum get me off the floor. They couldn't as the twins were hanging out. I couldn't move. The ambulance men carried me to the front room. I was in pain, holding onto my twins. They weren't moving. By the time the

midwife came, the twins were hanging on one cord. The midwife separated the babies from me and threw my babies into a grey bin. I felt total shame.

The entire street was looking on. My Dad was crying. Mum came with me in the ambulance. Peggy cleaned up the kitchen. Anne's baby was due in a month. She came to see me. Anne told me she had been my friend through school and wouldn't let me down now. She was brave. I gave Anne most of my baby things. One of my auntie's daughters was a midwife and sometimes worked on a children's ward. The pram went to her.
I stayed off work to get stronger and then went back. I blamed the experience on the Ouija board and the things I was into. I blamed myself. I blamed God too. Why did he do this?
It was at this time I said my first urgent prayer. "Please help me, God."
To this day I haven't messed with an Ouija board. In fact, the women at work threw the board away because it had frightened them.

A few months passed and Peggy died. We helped her family. She had always been there for me and my family. Peggy's family came from Glasgow. My Dad went and picked them up in his taxi from Manchester and did it free of charge. It didn't feel the same at work now that Peggy wasn't there.

Once again I decided to go to Eileen's at weekends. We started going out on Fridays to the town centre until 2am. We went to a night club. It was good. There was never any trouble3. We shared taxis. Eileen loved going out as she worked hard the rest of the time. Her fits weren't so bad as she had tablets. She only drank shandy and I would have an odd cider. We met Sue, who was my age, and her younger sister Ann.

I still did babysitting but not so much. I only worked on a Saturday night.
At Eileen's I met a lad who was younger than me. We started going out and we had a relationship. At first it wasn't serious.

16

Later on we started going out a lot more. He met my family and I met his.

My auntie told us to go to her house as she was poorly. I bought a picture for her. It was of a little girl with black hair. My aunt said it looked like me.

My auntie was lovely but couldn't have children of her own. She loved Robert going to her as he entertained her a lot. Auntie thought he was funny. He played the spoons for her and she danced. She was as daft as Robert at times. Auntie was a big woman, like my Mum, and she didn't stand any messing about though she had a soft heart.

Auntie got really poorly. When my boyfriend and I visited her she kept pointing to the picture. There were only a few weeks left till we married. We didn't have a home to go to. We thought we would have to live with either my parents or his. We thought of calling it off. I was pregnant our parents were pushing us into marriage.

My auntie died and left her house to my Mum. We moved in. It was illegal not to pay rent so Mum charged us £5 a week.

I went to a Methodist church with one of my aunts when my husband was at work. She was a lovely auntie and loved people. She made cakes for her church. I was also reading tea leaves and into spiritualism with another auntie.

My husband hated God and didn't go to church at all. Mum didn't go to any church. She had been hurt by Alice and so she stopped going.

I had some belief but didn't know what. I was confused.

When our baby Ryan was born my husband left me to organise the christening. Two years later, our second baby Gemma was born. Again, I did it all. The christenings were to get the children into church schools.

As our house had only one bedroom we had to move. We moved onto the Estate where I lived when I was younger. We knew people there and Mum was on the same street as us. Robert wasn't far, just round the corner. Eileen helped us. We soon made new friends. The children were at a nursery near our house. One day my husband was at work and I was going out. I got the pram on the path, put the break on and turned to get my purse. Ryan took the break off. Gemma went down the steps in the pram. Our neighbour came out and got Mum and the ambulance. Mum and Ryan, and the neighbour came with me and Gemma in the ambulance. Poor thing, Gemma needed stitches.

My husband was working in a night club called "Braces." Bobby Ball owned the club and he was funny.

My husband was on good money so we decided to buy a house. It was only five doors away from his work. The school was a two minute walk away. It was a church school and so the children went to Sunday school.

My husband started seeing other women. One evening, I got a friend to babysit for me. I got a taxi. I went into the pub where my husband was working. I got a pint and went and poured it over his disco decks. I got back in the taxi and went home. I thought he stopped seeing other women, but my friend saw him again and again with other women. This carried on for months. Eileen kept telling me to leave my husband, but didn't. I was thinking of my children. We had lots, but didn't have love, honesty or God. I was still into star reading and tea leaves because I thought it would make a difference. Our marriage ended in divorce. We divorced because of unreasonable behaviour and adultery.
We had been buying the house but I signed it over to my ex-husband. I could not afford payments as I was on benefits. He was working, so he could afford to pay the mortgage.

I had to move. I was on my own with my children. I had my records and CB radio for company.

The children stayed at the same school although it was a longer walk. Eileen and Mum helped me to get stuff. They bought some food and beds for the kids. I moved onto the same street as a babysitter I knew. When the babysitter friend died I missed her so much I decided to go and see a spiritualist. The spiritualist frightened me. I pushed her as she told me I would always be poor.

I started to write poems for something to do. I liked doing this as I'd done it at school.

About this time I met a girl who was good to me. She bought the kids lots of stuff. I started to have feelings for her. This ended as I knew where it was leading. I needed someone to keep me company. I needed to be loved.

I met a man through the CB radio who was fifteen years older and we became friends. I moved in with him. He had a two bedroom flat. He couldn't cope with my children as they also needed my attention. He was unable to have children of his own so was not used to kids. Our relationship ended in tears.

I had nowhere to go with the children so he let me stay in his flat until I got a new house. Sometimes he stayed at his friends so that I spent time with the children on my own.

I needed a place for me and my children so I went on his CB radio to ask people. No one knew of anywhere. I needed something quickly. I also had my name on the housing list but nothing was coming up. My Mum and Eileen didn't come as much. Dad still called. Sometimes I got very lonely. I'd go on the CB just to see who was listening. I heard people chatting. I also watched TV.

The children went to the church school together. When the children came home from school I met them at the bottom of the street. They were only six so my friend walked them half way for me. Sometimes Dad brought them home. On the days Dad brought them home I wrote poems about how I felt, I'd play records over the airwaves and read the stars out of the papers hoping that I'd find love someday.

Ryan played out on his bike and Gemma went to dancing classes. I was a bit better with my balance so I walked with her each

19

week. It took about twenty minutes to walk to the lessons. Gemma loved dancing. Mum had never left me alone, and so I never left my children alone. I always made Ryan come with us even though he didn't want to. Ryan brought his peddle bike and rode through the school while Gemma danced. I'd go the same way every week. I passed my friend's house. Sometimes I called in on the way back.

While waiting for a new house I got chatting to a lad on the CB radio. He had a brother John who was into the same music as me. I'd never met John though I heard his music in the back ground when I was on the CB radio.

Then one day, something happened on my way home from Gemma's dancing class. I passed my friend's house. I was day dreaming, thinking about getting the children bathed and then to bed. I was going to relax and watch TV.

A lad jumped out of the bushes.

"Are you Flower Bud?" he asked. I was startled by I replied.

"Sorry! I'm John. You chat to my brother on the CB radio."

"Sorry! I've got to get home. I'll call you later when I've got the children to bed."

That's what I did. John and I chatted for ages about music and other stuff. I asked him if he wanted me to read his stars. He told me he didn't believe in that stuff. He told me to burn my tarot cards. He told me about his life. I told him about mine. I never thought of the other people who could hear these things on the airwaves. John told me to pray for a house. Before I went to sleep I thought about, but I didn't pray.

The next night John shouted me again. I answered. He told me to meet him at his home for a brew. The next morning I got the kids off to school and told Dad to pick them up. I met John at his home for coffee and to share music.

His Mum opened the door. She told me to go upstairs. The first thing I thought was, "if he thinks he's going to try it on, he can think again."

I stepped into the bedroom and on his bed was a blue book. I realise it was a Bible on his pillow. I asked John if he was a Mormon.

He laughed, but not in a mocking way. He said, "I'm a born again Christian."
It meant nothing to me.
I sat on the chair in the bedroom and played music. We chatted for hours. John told me he used to drink but didn't any more. We went downstairs and he walked me home to the flat.

That night I couldn't stop thinking about John. It was like a magnet being drawn, but not in the same way as before. I kept thinking "Why didn't he make a pass at me? Why was he different from other men I'd met?" The day after, I called him once the kids had gone to school. He told me he had prayed for a house for me and that I should also pray for a house.
That night after the kids were in bed, I started to pray the Lord's Prayer. I knew it from school. I started to think of all the stuff I had done wrong. It wasn't at all right in my head.
The next day I took the children to school. When I got home there was a letter behind the door. It offered us a house. Wow! I thought, "Prayer works!" I was so excited I had to tell John. I asked him about prayer and why answers happened. John told me about God. I wanted to hear more and more. It was like magic. But the magic I'd had before was looking at the stars and going to a spiritualist.

I was desperate to move. I moved into a new house with no electricity or gas. I had a camping cooker, a candle, a table and a settee. Eileen bought me a twin tub washer and Mum bought me curtains. Three days later the electricity was turned on.
John worked at a security job and came to see me before he went to work. We were just friends. We swapped music. I would call him on the CB radio. We chatted for weeks. Then at weekends, John, his dog and records moved in. He took me to church. I came to know Jesus.
I wasn't allowed to take the children to church as their dad was still interfering. God had his way in the end. The children went to Sunday school. They loved it. Gemma still did dancing and Ryan came on with his bike as John worked nights.

21

I started to write poems about love and God. I also wrote about my life. I didn't go to spiritualist nights anymore. John told me about the dangers. John went to work and I'd sit at the CB radio and chat for a bit.

Some people, who I thought were friends, stole the radio from me. They swapped the back of it and then brought it back. It didn't even look like mine. We got rid of the radio because it caused problems. I only used it because I was lonely. I didn't need it any more. My past had gone.

I started to get closer to God. I made new friends in the churches of Rochdale. We got to know a lot of people through being involved in church life.

John had been living with me for a year. We both went to our pastor. He told us we had four weeks in which to marry. John had lost his job so didn't know if it was right to marry. That night we both went to bed and had the same vision. We saw little red eyes like frogs eggs on the ceiling. We didn't know it was a warning. We told our pastor we both wanted to marry. We both said we were sorry to God. We wanted to put it right. John and I honoured God with marriage. At that time I didn't realise I was pregnant although I didn't want to be pregnant at that time.

When we got married, we didn't have a thing. There was just ten pounds in our pocket. Both of us smoked and we needed fags. A lad ran off with our last tenner. We got married with nothing. Our friend Marilyn made our wedding cake and the ladies from the Aglow gave us money. My friend Sheila made my wedding dress. Her husband, Jim, drove the wedding car as Dad walked me down the aisle. For weddings, Dad always dressed his taxi nicely with white sheets on the seats and flowers and white ribbon. I used to help him do it. We had a holiday in a caravan in Wales. We were blessed.

When we got to the caravan I opened the wardrobe. There was £30 for us to spend. Mum had the kids for a week. When we came home and we were blessed again with food.

I started to fall a lot more. I didn't want John to know. Gemma would hold my hand and said nothing. A friend told us to go to

the doctors because I was falling over all the time. I saw a
specialist. I was told I had slight cerebral palsy. This was a
shock to both of us. I thought I'd been clumsy all my life. I
never thought of anything else. I remember Mum taking me to a
hospital when I was about five. I had to walk up and down. My
leg dragged and was twisted. They thought it would get better.
When I was born the doctors told Mum I wouldn't live because
I'd been short of oxygen. Again, when I was two months old,
Mum and Dad left me near a fire. The fumes from the calor gas
heater caused a shortage of oxygen. I was in hospital in an
oxygen tent. I survived! My God, he's a living God.
The cerebral palsy meant John had to stop work and become my
carer. It felt like grieving. I'd lost everything. I fell a lot more.
Previously, I'd held onto the pram when Ryan and Gemma were
small. It had been my stick.

Our son was born. We named him John, after his Dad. He was
born on his granddad's birthday, so it was a special day.
I had postnatal depression. I didn't want to know God. I
slammed the door in my friend's face, but she still came to see
me. I even threw good food in the bib. I threw the Christmas tree
with its lights across the room. I was crying and then laughing.
God was with me still, but I wasn't with God. He loved me
through it all. God never leaves you or forsakes you. I just
wanted to be alone. I would go to Mum's on my own.
Sometimes I took Gemma and left baby John with my husband.

Our house was huge so we were able to have Bible studies and
praise nights at home. Our friends came along. Bikers also came.
There were some local lads who threw stones at the pram and
called us "Bible bashers."
A rough family lived over the road and stole milk off our
doorstep every day. They hassled us. The pastor told us to pray
all night about it. We played worship music and prayed and
opened our curtains. They did a moonlight flit!
That's when I knew God worked and saw the power of prayer.
The woman who moved into the empty house needed it all done
up. The previous people had wrecked the stairs. It was a mess! I

asked the new lady to come over for a cup of tea. We got friendly with the young woman. In the summer, once we got our kids in bed we would sit on the doorstep talking till midnight. We had tea and cake.

When we had our second son Joel, I found a mums and toddlers group at the local school. I was only a two minute walk, so I'd go twice a week. John sometimes came with me and brought me back. As I had the pram I was able to hold onto it. It helped me to keep my balance.
Sometimes my two older children went to their dad's. HE didn't have them a lot and it caused trouble. When the children were older, Gemma left me and went to live with her dad.

A week after Gemma left, my Mum died. I didn't even know Mum was in hospital. My niece didn't tell me until the day before Mum died.
I became depressed again.
I was the last to know anything about my relatives. They always kept me in the dark. Only Eileen and dad came to see us. None of my other relatives ever visited us. John's Mum came round. My niece and I weren't close. She always preferred Robert as they both had bikes. My cousin never came, neither did her relatives. When the bill for the funeral came, we had to pay for it. None of the family helped. The relatives spent all Mum's savings. I only got her watch and that got pinched.
Our church paid the bill. God always provides for us. He never lets us down. We had friends in the church. John's Mum never missed coming. She was so nice. John's Mum has done a lot for me and still does.

The following year Dad was really ill. Ryan went to live with him.

We stayed for a year or two more in our house because we had good friends and didn't want to leave. In the end we moved for two reasons. Firstly, some lads on the street hassled us.

Secondly, the house was too big for us. We decided to get a flat. I had started to fall a lot more. I fell down the stairs twice.

We always wanted what others had so we were always short of money. We got into debt. The bailiffs were due to come. My friend came and paid the debt for us. On both sides of our families there were financial curses. We needed to break these curses. My Mum was always short of money. John's Mum always used hand-me-down clothes for our children instead of being short of food.
One day I went shopping with my last pound. I always walked looking down because I had to concentrate on my balance. I prayed as I walked. On the ground I saw a twenty pound note in the bush!! I was thanking God all the way home! This happened a couple of times.

God Encounter

Once we decided to move to a flat we put our name on the housing list. It didn't matter which part of Rochdale we moved to. We were involved with several churches so we knew people indifferent parts of the town. We would settle in a church near to where we moved. We got a small two bedroomed flat in Littleborough, near a small church. We knew the pastor. His name was Alan.

We said goodbye to our friends and moved. Our friend Brenda helped us settle in.

John Junior went to a church school and Joel went to the playgroup at the Methodist Church.

About a week later after moving, we went to the nearby church. We met old friends and made new. Alan picked me up for prayer meetings. John got involved with evangelism. We did a lot of outreach on the Estate. We prayed for people together.

John likes drums and got drumming. We went to a church that had lots of bikers. Some of the bikers came to our flat and brewed up. They left their bikes in the garden. Our boys loved it and sat on the bikes. I was on another prayer team. John went out with the bikers Gemma came to see us. She had grown up and realised it wasn't all bad with us. She had come through some things herself. Ryan didn't come to see us much.

My Dad died. It was the same again. I had nothing. The other relatives had his money and bought new bikes. I was left out again. Now I realised my treasures are with God. I was grateful for friends who I could turn to Gemma and Eileen were the only ones who came to see us. John would walk Gemma to the bus stop afterwards. John's Mum lived near so I could see her at any time.

Robert went to live with his son, Little Robert.

I continued with church life and made friends. People came during the day when the kids were at school. Our flat was an open door. Anyone who wanted a chat came. We had a speaker come once a month. One time Gideon Bibles were given out.

There was a communal garden and the boys played in it. One day Joel came in screaming. On his head was a pizza. Someone had thrown it out of the flat above. The pizza had landed on Joel's head.

One day John and I got on a bus. There were only two seats left, so I sat down and John went and sat next to a lad. He was a bit rough. He had an army jacket on and a bit of a beard. He got off at the same stop as us. The next week as we came out of church we saw the lad we had seen on the bus. He stopped and asked us where we had been. John told him we'd been at church and were on our way home.
During the week, Dot had rung me asking me to pray for a lad who had moved into a flat near her. We always prayed for these types of people. Dot had a heart for them and so did we. Little did we know that it was the same lad we had met on the bus. The following week, Dot brought the lad to church. We sat on the same row of seats with our boys. The next night, the lad got up for prayer.John asked him to talk to Noel Protctor. The lad committed himself to God. His name was Barry Woodward. Barry now goes round sharing God. He has a charity which reaches out to drug addicts and tells them about Jesus.
Barry is now married. He never thought he'd do this. We still see Barry and love him lots.
When Barry was in training he spoke at a tent mission where lots of Rochdale churches were involved. We went to see him. Barry had grown a lot in the things of God.
At the tent mission they were short of a drummer. John drummed. He was asked to play the drums. He used two packs of extra strong mints as drumsticks! They worked. We ate the mints afterwards.

John also got involved with a rehab centre. John shared about Jesus. We got friendly with one of the lads who became a

Christian. John baptised him. He still knows God. We see him now and again.

We got involved with the Business Men's Fellowship. That's where John was healed from stomach ulcers.

We became friendly with our local radio station. It was based in the hospital grounds. I listened to it a lot. We invited them to have a live programme from our flat. We asked them to come and see us. I read a poem over the air. My friend heard it in the doctor's surgery. It was a chance to mention God. Brenda rang in and asking for requests. It was fun! The radio programmers came at 7am for a breakfast show. We set it up in our small flat. The lads from the radio station were a laugh. They had our sons dancing for them before they went to school.

We also went to the studio. They interviewed us. It was good. Through this, we had some of our church friends go to the studio and sing worship songs.

I still went to the Women Aglow meetings. John was involved with evangelism and I was involved in prayer meetings. Barry went to Bible College and Dot still came round to pray with me.

The flat got a bit too small as the boys got older so we thought about moving to a three bedroomed house. We had looked around and waited on God but nowhere came up. The boys were in a small bedroom with bunk beds. We put our name on the housing list again and got an offer three months later.

The house was in Manchester on a big estate. We needed to view it. As we took our boys to school we told them we'd be back in time to collect them at the end of the day. They were only eight at the time. My balance was bad and we needed to move. We had decided to move and that was it. Our pastor told us not to go, but we didn't listen. We were thinking our flat was too small and our children needed more space. We thought it was right. We knew we had to leave family and friends.

Grass is Greener

We got on the bus. It must have taken at least an hour and a half to get there. A man met us and took us round the house. It had huge gardens back and front. There were toilets downstairs and upstairs. It was just what we wanted. It would be alright for me. We met the man of the house at the door. He was in a wheelchair. He was nice. His wife had crutches. They shook hands and told us the neighbours were fine. We agreed to take the house, signed the papers and moved in.
We got the local paper to find details of a local school and church.
I knew someone who went to the Women's Aglow so I contacted her. She picked me up for meetings once a month.
The boys' school was round the corner. It was really rough. The boys were picked on a lot. They came home crying and with nose bleeds.
We found a church. It was small but had lovely people. John did outreach work for them.

We unpacked our stuff and a few days later invited the next door neighbours in for a brew and cakes. They were really nice people. They watched the boys playing in the back garden while I washed up.

One day John took Joel to the doctors. While there, John passed out. John rang me from the hospital. John was passing a stone. I didn't have any money. The lady next door told me to get a taxi. She gave me her purse full of money. I went to the hospital and back with the money. She said she trusted us because she saw something good in us. John came out of hospital and was alright. It was nice of her to do this, so John got her flowers for her kindness.
One time we shared our photos with them, and they did with us. They both liked us. They had lived on the street for twenty years but had never done this before. I gave her a booklet of my poems.

The neighbours on the other side were totally different. They were really noisy. They had parties until four in the morning. We approached them about this but got abuse back.

People came in one night and we heard a gun fire. Another time they installed a toilet in the bathroom at five in the morning. They came and asked us to fill their kettle and use our toilet! When we went out they called and shouted after us as we walked down the road. I rang a friend and she prayed with me. I cried.

One day John was in Manchester with the World Wide Tribe. The neighbours opened the door, got a lad and hung him over my fence. The lad was bleeding from his head. The ambulance came but he was dead when it arrived. The police were there. In fact they never seemed to be away from the house. The police came to us. We acted dumb. We didn't want to be seen as grassers.

I started to write about my life. I also wrote poems. I didn't blame God I blamed ourselves.

In spite of hating the area, Gemma kept coming to visit. Eileen and Brenda also came. No matter where we lived they came to see us. John's Mum lived in Manchester, near John's brother, so we saw her there, to get away from it all.

There were gangs on the street corners. Girls as young as ten were in cars racing up and down. Our boys couldn't play out as they might get run over. It made me more unsettled and insecure. I started to get down and too frightened to go out. I lost my confidence and my walking got worse.

We went to church but older people didn't because they were frightened to walk down the street.

I wished and prayed I'd never moved here. I was frightened. We needed to move somewhere else.

I bought a paper and we found a private landlord in Gorton. There was a three bedroomed house. It had a large living room. We took the house without looking at it.

We moved in. When we went upstairs the windows were a bit damp. We bleached them. The boys had their own bedrooms at last. The boys had had bunk beds so we separated them.

We settled in and found a new school for the boys. It was a bit better than the last school. It was a small church school.

We made friends with an older lady who had a daughter with special needs.

I got the local phone book to find a church. I rang one church. It was an African church. John went to introduce himself at the church. He was away for hours. I thought something was wrong. I put the kettle on and started to pray. When John arrived he was with the pastor and his wife.

They asked if they could pray round the house. They stopped under the stairs. There was some tarot cards! We burned them. John joined the worship team as a drummer. The church had bought a new drum but had no one to play it. I joined the prayer team and helped the children's group. I struggled walking but they always held my hand to keep me steady. We went to church early and prayed for an hour before the service. There was praise and worship for three hours a week. It was brilliant! We loved the music so we enjoyed the worship. We loved the culture of praising God. One time we worshipped all night! The music sounded like soul music. I was used to the Supremes, Gladys Knight and the Pips, so I loved the sounds.

On Sundays we worshipped for two hours and then got into the Word for another hour.

Our boys were white and had skinheads. The little ones laughed at them. The boys were in dramas and loved the singing. Joel sang a lot. Young John liked drumming, like his Dad. The women loved us. We had African tops and wore them.

Gemma still came to see us and so did Eileen. Eileen brought us food and sweets. Eileen didn't want to know God and neither did Gemma at that time. Gemma had wanted to know God when she was little. John had baptized her when she was seven. Ryan never came to the house. He had never been baptized. He knew God when we first met John. Ryan never came after he left home and went to live with Robert.

31

Our kitchen needed painting so we did it. We didn't see the landlord much. He charged us £500 a month which was alright. One day we got locked out. The pastor had his tribal gear and came and helped us. The pastor broke the door for us to get in and then bought a new door.

Then we decided to decorate the bedrooms. Joel and John had to share rooms till we finished. John went upstairs when Eileen was there. He pulled the paper off, and off came the plaster too! We rang the landlord. He told us we needed to pay for the repairs because it was our fault. He also told us he needed an extra £500 for the windows. I told him to get lost.
A week or two passed and there was no word from the landlord. He owned a pub somewhere. That's all we knew about him. Our church tried to help us. They did most of the work. The boys were in the same room for weeks.
One day a friend from church knocked on the door. We prayed about the situation. We needed money which we didn't have. We stayed up and prayed all night with our pastor and his wife. I thought, praying worked once, it will work again.

The landlord came round and found out we were having African friends visit. He went mad. We found out that he was a gang member of the EDL.
The landlord gave us two weeks to get out. He wanted us out for 7th April. God had to do something. We got an offer of a two bedroom house in Rochdale so we took it. We would be near John's Mum and Robert.

In the meantime, Gemma was seeing a lad and needed us. It was Mother's Day. We had been to church and got a call from Gemma. She had lost her baby. We needed to get back for her. Gemma's Dad had his own life and his new wife. Gemma and her step mother didn't get on. My friend at church prayed with me.

The church in Gorton gave us a blessing and told us we were a wonderfully blessed family.

We didn't blame God for the tough time in Manchester. It wasn't his fault. We had gone out of his will.

We moved on 7th April. The landlord wanted his money but we didn't give him any, and he didn't give us our bond either. We found out two years later, when watching telly that the house was 'unreasonable' and it had to be demolished. It had rats and was unsafe to live in.

God's timing is right. We got back to Rochdale at the time my daughter needed us. Gemma and I bonded again. Over the years, Gemma's Dad hadn't wanted us to see her. He had given us a lot of grief. It made me see that God looks after his own. We have to go through difficult things in life and this was one thing where we needed God with us.

We were back in Rochdale, where I was born. It felt a bit rough but it was a start.

We didn't look for a church the first week back. There was a show in Rochdale, about the Easter message. We went. We both cried all the way through. The fact of being loved and cared for again met our needs. We needed our friends and family. We had been in the wilderness while in Manchester.

John's Mum had missed us. She lived nearby. Robert and Ryan lived round the corner. Our old friends came to visit.

We needed a church. We went back to the one where we had got married, but it didn't feel right. John started to look for another church. I stayed home with the boys on Sundays. John had been to every church except one. He knew the pastor at this last church. John got up on the Sunday morning and said, "Come on! We are all going." We only had a fiver left. We got a taxi.

We got into the church. It was so warm and welcoming. The leaders took us to the back room and prayed with us. The boys quickly settled into Sunday school. John got involved in worship and evangelism and I went to prayer meetings.

The boys went to a small school about a twenty minute walk away. They didn't get into trouble at all. It was the new start that the boys needed. They needed stability. The boys' bedroom was small so they had the bunk beds again. They needed more space. They were always arguing but we needed to stay so that they settled in school and church.

We hadn't been at the church long when we got invited to go away with them for a weekend. We did. We met Brenda and Anna. They had some free time and so I went with them. John went with the lads. Brenda and Anna took me to the swimming pool. I made an excuse not to go in. Ever since I had been thrown in the water at school I was frightened of it. The girls took me by the hand. They got me in the children's pool first. I loved it. John was panicking. He wondered if I would be safe. The following year we went away for a weekend again. This time I went in the big pool. Our son John learnt to swim. Joel was frightened. I'd passed my fear of water onto him. I told Joel it was alright and that it was safe to come with me.

The pool was the same depth all over. I didn't swim. I just jumped up and down. I ran in the pool. I did things in the pool I couldn't do anywhere else. I was free! John saw another side of me. I was free and full of joy, laughing all the time in the pool. I played like a child. Our son John joined me, throwing me round in the pool. That was when I wanted to learn to swim.

My friend took me to the baths. After four weeks of getting used to the deep end I swam in a circle. My left side was weaker than my right!

After about six weeks I let go of the side. There was an instructor who saw me. He taught the Manchester para Olympic swimmers. He told me to swim with him. I looked up and told God it was for Him. I swam the length of the pool. The instructor told me not to look to my right or left, just to keep my eyes on the instructor. This was also prophetic.

I didn't obey, and a lad who jumped in front of me made me panic. The instructor picked me up. I finished the length. I achieved it! I love water. It's pure and simple but it can heal.

The street was rough. Cars raced about. The boys stayed in the garden to play. We made friends. There were other kids was same age near us.

The lads on the street put petrol rags through our letterbox. We got called names again but we tried to stick in there. Eileen came round when John was out at night. John was training as a Street Pastor and went to Manchester once a month. He went on the streets near where we used to live.

We tried to move out many times but didn't manage. The street gangs got too much for us. My walking got worse and I needed John's help more.

John joined a group called Psalm Drummers and did a lot of drumming. He was also drumming for a group called Freedom.

One day when we went to Manchester we heard drumming on the street. John bought a drum with his last bit of money and came home with it. John heard rattling in the drum! An old lady from church told me to get John to empty the drum. We prayed with our friend who came round. We cut the drum open and out came this burning smell. Our friend told us that when people kill men and women in Africa they torment them with banging on the drums. We got rid of the drum and prayed over our house. The drum had been used for tribal stuff.

John made sure he had brand new drums after that and only brought them from shops.

The boys slept out at weekends. It was good for them to get away from the street.

I went to the local Women's Aglow group. I became membership chairman and prayer chairman.

John and I got involved with more things while waiting to move. God always looked after us even though it was rough. It made us stronger in our faith.

We went to Bible studies and prayer meetings. The boys were looked after.

At least being in council property we had no problems with the landlord. It was a temporary stop. We needed three bedrooms. This time we were more stable and we weren't running.

My walking was slower. I still fell but my strength in God was stronger. People from other church came to see us and we were able to share our story. I decided to write more poems. They weren't just about God. John saw a competition in a Christian paper. I wrote a poem which won. That's when I started writing for God.

Darkness into Light

We looked round the area and found a house for rent. I always carried pen and paper with me so I jotted down the address. The next day we rang about it. We had told our church friends about the house and they prayed with us. The agency told us we could view it the next day. They took our details. A little later the agent phoned back and told us we couldn't have it because we were unemployed. Someone else was looking at the property. We prayed and prayed.

The following day the agent rang and asked us if we wanted the house. We were told the couple had turned it down. We needed an employed guarantor to sign for us. Our friend came and did this. We moved in two months later.

Brenda helped us move. She helped me wash our kitchen. Other friends also helped.

John's Mum lived round the corner and so did Robert. Ryan had married so Robert lived on his own.

I continued at Women's Aglow and helped at a Mums and Toddlers group each week. It was held at church. Brenda looked after the children and I talked to the mums. An elderly lady called Elsie sat in another room and prayed all the time. I learned from her. We did this for about three years. We stopped when the children started school and no one else joined.

We made friends with our next door neighbours. They were lovely. She always made us laugh. They knew we were Christians but didn't want to know God themselves. They left their keys with us when they went away. We turned the lights on for them. One time we had a big garden party and invited everyone from the street. Some people from other churches came. We got the drums out. The two from next door started dancing. It was funny!

I had my first experience of the power of prayer. Some people prayed about my legs. My leg straightened and grew! This was prayer! The Holy Spirit is real. Yes, I still struggled and John was my carer but God was in control.

I am reminded of what the Bible says when Jesus healed a crippled lady.
When Jesus saw her, he called her forward and said to her, "Woman, you are set free from your infirmity."

The boys didn't have to move school. In fact it was nearer for them. The house was in an Asian community. The boys soon made friends.
John fixed the children's bikes. John knew about bikes. We had a small garage where John was able to fix up bikes for our boys. He bought himself a small scooter to get around on. I had a disabled scooter.
When we went to the park, the boys and John were on peddle bikes and I was on my scooter. Well, if you saw us – I had the tennis racquets in front of my legs and the cans of pop in the front basket.

John only went on his scooter to visit people or go to the shops. John and I went dancing on soul nights. We still loved music. We had met through music, we loved music and we still do.
Our boys loved music too. Joel played drums and sang. He also wrote songs. Young John loved music but didn't write songs. He liked rapping and played worship songs. They both played the drums and did concerts for Rochdale Psalm Drummers. They drummed in front of big crowds. Neither of them was shy.

Our landlord was alright. We didn't see him much because we had to deal with the estate agents. After five years, the agent told us we needed to move. The landlord wanted to sell the house. Joel was twelve and John was fourteen.

We put our name on the housing list but nothing was coming up. We carried on at church. They kept praying with us about the situation.
One day our friends John and Chris Nuttall asked us if we had found anywhere to live. We hadn't. John took us to his parents' house. He told us to look round and left us there for an hour. We had a brew and prayed together. When John returned he asked if

we wanted to stay for about twelve months until we found somewhere else.

We said, "Yes,"

It was a huge three bedroom house. It was so beautiful. We met all the family including their daughter Emma. I really grew close to Emma. She is so lovely and caring.

We needed a nearby school for Joel. We kept John at the same school because he could get the bus.

Before this, Eileen became really ill. We saw her and within three months she had died. I was so shocked. She was a big woman, yet she went down so quickly in size. This was the hardest thing I had come across. I'd loved her more than anyone. She had looked after me and brought me up. It took a few years for me to come to terms with this loss.

Once again my relatives hadn't told me Eileen had cancer of the bones. I needed to forgive my niece. So I had ministry at the church. I felt free even though I didn't tell my niece.

Some words that helped me at the time were:

For with you in the fountain of life; in your light we see light.

"I removed the burden from their shoulders; their hands were set free from the basket."

Gemma, Robert, Ryan and John's Mum continued to visit us. After Eileen died, her husband gave us her dog, Jack. I thought I would keep falling over him and that he would bite. But Jack was very gentle. We loved him. He followed me everywhere. John and Chris didn't mind us having Jack at the property. Jack loved Joel.

Caterpillar into a Butterfly

When I first met John he took me to a butterfly farm. It was so beautiful. The butterflies were flying round me, over me and settling on me. I just stood in awe and didn't want to leave. The more I stood still, the more the butterflies settled on me. It was like I could see myself just receiving freedom and being filled with peace and love. In a similar way, the more you keep still and wait on God the closer he comes to you.

At first the caterpillar hides in the bushes, but at the right time it changes into a beautiful butterfly. Each butterfly is so different and unique. There are so many different colours. I thought of myself as a butterfly. I had been a slow and very shy caterpillar, but now I was a butterfly. I was now free and unique. We are all unique in God's eyes. I am free to worship, free to speak, I am free from hurts and pain in my heart. God has turned my sorrow into joy.

I don't want to see caterpillars in the bush. I want to see the butterflies free to fly. I don't want to go back to the bushes and be trapped with shyness. I want to be free like the butterflies. God saw me and chose me to tell others my story. Each of us has talents. God gives talents to each of us.

In the meantime, Gemma had met a lad who was in the army with Ryan. Gemma told us she was moving to Belfast. My heart felt empty. At first I was worried, but I had to let her go. She was only twenty one. We went with Gemma on the boat to Ireland. The journey took eight hours and it was good. I cried all the way home. Gemma was there for three years. When she came back, it was to get married.

It was Gemma's wedding and she didn't want her Dad there. She had a bad relationship with him. Gemma chose me to walk her down the aisle. I felt so honoured. The day before the wedding it rained really hard. The ground was soaked. We got all the churches together to pray. On the wedding day, the sun came out and the grass dried up.

All the girls came to our house, and the boys went to Gemma's house.

Since John was Scottish, Gemma wanted kilts worn at the wedding. When she was young she often said she loved kilts. Gemma also said she had a surprise for all of us at the wedding. She had ordered a piper and hadn't told us. When she was walking down the aisle we heard the pipes.

Gemma got married at an Anglican Church and went there for a while after her marriage. She had been used to our kind of church which she called "happy-clappy-Pentecostal-two-step."

One week she went to an induction service at the church where she had been baptized. From then on she went to the Baptist church. Gemma and her husband are now deacons at the church.

Robert moved to Chorley near to my son John and his children. Linda, my niece, has spoken to me because I learned to forgive. It was after this that Linda introduced me to a niece I'd never seen.

When I was two years old, Eileen had a baby girl who had to be adopted. Linda had met her sister a lot of times but never introduced me to her. This doesn't matter because through forgiving, I now have two nieces! God always gives you more than you expect! There's more to come. Blessings I don't know about yet.

It wasn't twelve months that we stayed in the Nuttall's house, but five years. John and Chris needed to sell the house. We needed to move again. The boys had left home. The house had got too big for us. Young John stayed in various places – sometimes with friends and sometimes with his girlfriend. Sometimes he came to see us. He went through a rebellious stage in his teenage years.

Joel still visited. One day we were all going to the town centre. Joel had come for dinner and we decided to go to the chippy for tea. We needed to cross the road. The road was clear. Joel crossed. We waited and crossed half way. A car came from nowhere. Joel put his head down and we prayed like never before! John and I clung to each other. The force of the car moved us but we didn't go off balance. The angels were by our side. I thanked God for his protection. Once across the road I sat on a bench. I was shaking but relieved we were alive.

We put our names down for a council bungalow but we weren't old enough.

There was sheltered housing near where we used to live and it was near John's Mum. We put our name down for one of the flats. The only problem was we weren't old enough for these either. God had other plans. We rang the housing manager who told us that because I was disabled we could have a flat. We went to view the flats. We waited, but there was no phone call. I thought we had no chance of getting a flat because there were five others ahead of us on the waiting list. A friend of ours lived in the flats. She went up stairs to the empty flat, laid her hands on it and prayed that we would get the flat. Soon afterwards we got a phone call to say that one person was viewing the flat but if they refused it we would be offered it. I rang Norma and asked her to pray for us again. Two days later we got another call asking us to view the flat. We viewed it and took it.

Our friend, John, from another church, hired a van. We moved in. We had to give a lot away because we were moving from a three bedroom house to a one bedroom flat.

We soon made new friends. There's a big lounge in the sheltered accommodation where we meet at night. We have meals together. A month later, John's Mum moved to the same complex. We keep an eye on each other. Since being in our present accommodation we have put on sixties nights and got dressed up. We have had computer classes. I learned how to use a laptop. Before that we had a desk top. It was simple and had no internet access. The lessons were free. I taught a woman how to use a laptop. She bought one and now goes on it a lot to play games and use Facebook. We had chair exercises. That was fun! It was free to us because the council paid for it. When the funds ran out, the lessons stopped. I gave the lady instructor some of my poems before she left.

John can go out and I feel safe here. Our Mum is also here. We meet in the lounge and have supper together. It's fun. There's a man in here who has a very short memory. He was a wrestler in his younger days. He's lovely. He knows John though.

We sit outside in the summer. We talk, share, drink and eat chocolate. There's quite a bit of gossiping goes on but we don't get involved. We like everyone. Peoples' ages range from fifty to one hundred years young. The manager has told us that we have brought sunshine to the place. We have a laugh with some of the residents. Others are hard to get on with, but I try my best to be friendly with them all.

We know the local taxis as my Dad drove one for years. We ring and they know us. Wherever we go I have shared Jesus with them.

Yes I'm still bad at walking and I've got a Zimmer trolley, but I'm safe. I am filled with joy and laugh about it. I'm off my trolley but not on my trolley. The joy of the Lord is my strength. John has fulfilled his dream of being a Street Pastor. They are now working in Rochdale, even more amazing is it on the estate where we live. We prayed for this.

John kept being asked to help at a church near where we live. I didn't want to move churches because of my friends. We kept coming and going. In the end I went with John to the local church – and we joined! Our friends from the previous church blessed us as we left. We are in fact part of the one church – the body of Christ.

At our new church we both do God's work. John evangelises and I lead prayer meetings. I have joined an intercession team and a connect team. We are both involved in connecting to people who are lost and need God.

I also belong to the Street Pastor's Prayer Team and pray for UCB via e-mails.

I have now learned about Jesus as my saviour and my friend. He loves every one of us. At school I knew about God but I didn't know Jesus as my Lord. Jesus Christ is the same yesterday and today and for ever. I've been healed and set free. I know I can do all things because Jesus gives me strength.

Isaiah 61:1 says, "The Spirit of the Sovereign Lord is on me because he has anointed me to preach good news to the poor... to proclaim freedom for the captives and release for the prisoners." I do this in prayer and by writing.

Here are some words people have spoken over me:
- God knows all your plans.
- You are an overcomer.
- You are wise, a woman of God who makes a difference.
- You will see healings and do healings.

All my skills and talents are from God. I still can't spell, but God looks at my heart. We are called to serve. God created me to be creative. God's not finished with me yet.

My past is past. When I sat in the tunnel all those years ago at school, God sent Anne to sit with me. He saw me, and it was as though he sat with me.
When the cooker fell on me, God saved me. He was underneath with me, protecting me.
About my twins, I know that when I get to heaven they will be there waiting. The reason I didn't see them was because God took them. I wasn't ready for them. I didn't see it that way at the time.
God saw my hurt and pain. He took all my shame. The curses have gone. He gives me blessings. His promises are in his Word, the Bible. God has protected me all the time.

One time when I was going to Oldham to speak at a women's group, someone was throwing fireworks from across the road. They were going over our heads. My friend took my hand. The Bible says "when you walk through fire, you will not be burned." We are covered by the blood of Jesus.

So now, I don't want to turn my life back. I have been through many things but not once has Jesus left me.

John is still my carer. My children come to visit us. We have got friends all over Rochdale and beyond.

Sometimes we go and listen to Barry. Through Barry we have brought a young girl to know God. She now works in Barry's office. Another lad who John brought to God is getting married this year. John is going to be his best man.
We also pray for a church in Manchester that works amongst street girls and others with addictions. We keep in touch via Facebook. There's a girl I met through Facebook who I brought back to God.

One day I was praying for the Street Pastors for an hour. I thought, "Right God, I don't want much. Please can I have a laptop?" Ten minutes later Barry came with one! I was amazed! That was the fastest my prayers have been answered.
The longest answer took twelve years. That was for an automatic washer instead of a twin tub.
Prayer has been important all my Christian life. John first taught me to pray. He also told me to write poems. Here are some of my poems. The poems have been published in different books. One poem has been published twice. I can't put all my poems in this book, but these are a few about my life.

My Kind of Magic
I used to look at my stars
It was all about money and fast cars.
Then I went to tarot reading
I thought it was a magic feeling.
Oh no! It's not true.
No wonder I was feeling blue.
She said, "You will always be poor."
I told her, "You silly woman." Then shut the door.
Now that kind of magic has gone
Because Jesus took it. Thank God there's none.
The Holy Spirit, I feel in me.
The magic of Jesus I can now see.
The magic of Satan I don't like
So I told him to take a hike.

Sadness and Gladness
I had a baby, a baby boy.
What a feeling! Oh what a joy!
A month or two later I was depressed.
My life was so busy I couldn't rest.
I threatened my loved ones, threw food in the bin.
I cried all day, what a horrible din.
I cried through Christmas, I didn't know why.
When they asked a reason, I couldn't reply.
And then I found Jesus and learned he loved me,
He showed me such love and he set me free.
Each day I thank God for what he has done.
He did it for me. My depression has gone.

Love Is
Love is like a flower
Growing stronger by the hour.
Love is like a butterfly
In your lovely big blue sky.
Love can bring sorrow and pain.
Love is always in my brain.
Love is there all the time.

Thank you God, for being mine.
Love can be laughter,
Happy ever after.
Love can bring tears.
Love breaks fears.
But love – you can't buy it with gold
Because, love is found and never sold.

Always There
You're always there to lend a hand.
You're always there to understand.
And you are there when I feel rough
And always there when things get tough.
You're always there when I'm feeling sad
And always there when we are glad.
You're wanted
You are loved
You really do care

(This poem was also turned into a song.)

It was one of my dreams to write poems. Another dream was to
learn to swim and I achieved it. Another dream I have is to ride a
white horse and hold on to its reigns. I'll get off the horse and
start preaching.
We all have dreams and hopes. Jesus grants you these hopes.
A verse in the Bible says, "For I know the plans I have for you,
says the Lord, plans to prosper you and not to harm you, plans to
give you hope and a future." The magic I had before I met John
wasn't right. God showed me the right path. God can do the
same for you. All I needed to do was to ask Jesus into my life.
Jesus is waiting for you to give your life to him. Jesus said, "I am
the way, the truth and the life. No man comes to the Father but
through me."

If you have been touched by my story you can contact me at Kirkholt Community Church in Rochdale. If you want to know more about what Jesus can do for you please come and talk to me. If God can do it for me, he can do it for you.
All you need is to believe and receive. Then you can achieve great things.

Printed in Great Britain
by Amazon

19316464R00031